Henri, Baby & Coco, Wainscott. Christmas

THE
CATWALK
CATS

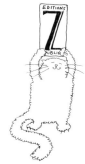

Drawings & Dialogue
GRACE CODDINGTON

Photographs
DIDIER MALIGE

Art Director
DANKO STEINER

Introduction
SALLY SINGER

Editor
MICHAEL ROBERTS

Coordinator
MICHAL SAAD

Cover Design by Michael Roberts
Santa Claus: Joe Harding. Polaroid by Tom Klectecka

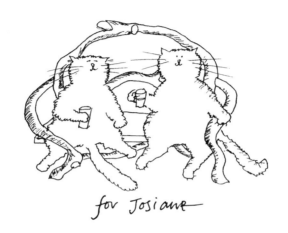

for Josiane

Bart, West 11th Street. Spring

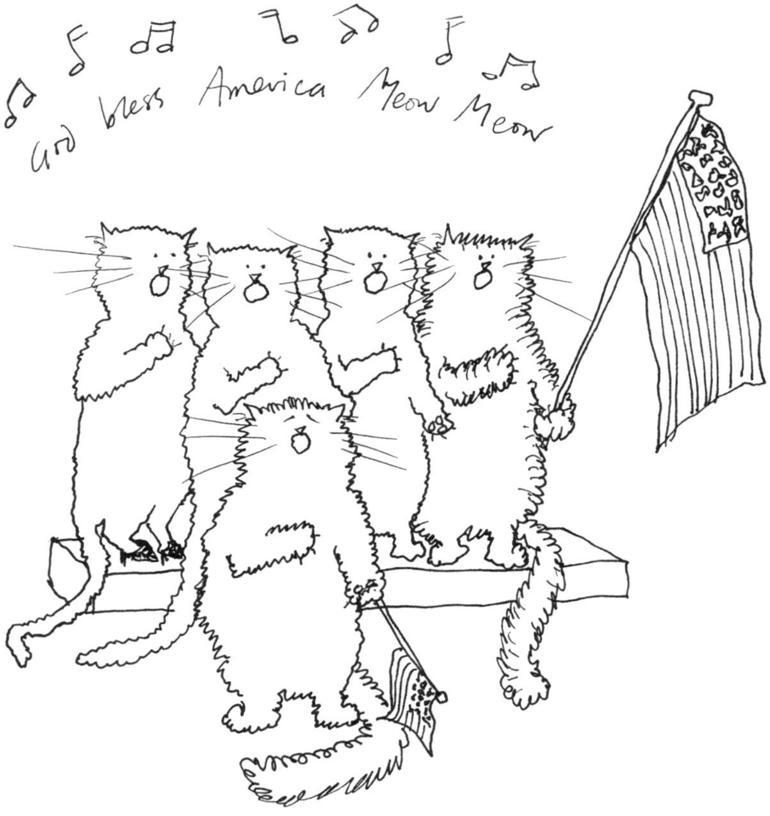
God bless America Meow Meow

"Mother" & Puff, Wainscott. Winter

I love your outfit Coco but I really
don't think they will allow you to wear
high heels to play in the U S open.....

CONTENTS

W hen Mother and Father suggested one night at Zutto over salmon sushi that I should write the introduction to this family album, my first cat-thought was to wriggle out of it. But you must understand that there I had no right of refusal: my mother is Grace Coddington, Creative Director of American *Vogue*;

my father is Didier Malige, a traveling groomer who wishes he could have been a Golden Gloves champion. They only "suggest," never demand, but their suggestions are ironclad and iron-fisted. This is one of the secrets to their success. Ask Anna Wintour.

Anyway, why me?

I'm not the most senior puss in the house—most certainly not. That would be Henri; he's the sort of old-school Felix who likes to surf with photographer David Sims in Montauk and have far-out, catnip-induced discussions with Bruce Weber's elephants. A poet philosopher, really. (Henri's a chartreux, and being French helps.) Moreover, I'm not really interested in the catwalk, even if it is the family stamping ground. All front-rowish territory I cede, whenever possible, to Coco and Baby because, bless them, they care. Coco (my girl, but that's another story) could not be happier than when she's perched backstage at Chanel, pre-show, and Lady Harlech is pawing her new collar. Coco just loves to reminisce about the season where we all witnessed the comeback of statement coats, or the time the feathers were flying at Tom Ford's Gucci. Whatever. (She's also a chartreux—Henri's sis, actually—and, again, being French helps.) Baby's a bon vivant who lives for shoes and bags and baubles because she's not exactly sample size. Maybe if she wasn't such a bon vivant with a taste for carbs, things would be different. She, too, is chartreux; and you can forget all that nonsense about how chats don't get fat. (No, being French hasn't helped.) Finally, I'm not the most beloved. That honor goes to Bart, the actual baby of

the family, whom everyone showers with attention. He's a blue Persian and has one of those ridiculously squashed-up mugs that visually minded types just "love, Love, LOVE."

But back to this book and who should pen it. Here's the whole ball of yarn: My mother, my father, my fellow felines are all

Coco & Puff, NYC. Spring

very, very "fashion," which means they don't do words, they do pictures. Father may read anything and everything (although we prefer to see him with a battered copy of something by chartreux-adoring Colette), and Mother adores Françoise Sagan (Meow, Tristesse!), but at the end of the day their minds drift to f-stops and frocks. I, on the other hand, am not at all "fashion." First, there's the matter of my beginnings. No idea who my parents were, or how I came by my red tabby good looks. Father saw me in a local pet store one day and thought my ginger coat was very Grace. Then they both came by to have a look, two shaggy Europeans in black go-

anywhere Prada crombies. I snoozed, fluffily and seductively, in a corner of the window. Smitten, they scooped me up—I purred triumphantly!—and carried me home to West Eleventh Street. So I didn't have a pedigree? Who cared? I was like one of

those anonymous items of clothing that
have just the right look but a label that
means nothing. At the end of the day it's
all about the look. (And wasn't I lucky?
Only Grace Coddington has spent the
last 30 years plucking redheads from the
runway chorus. Just call me Puff, the Happy Hoofer.)

But in the end, I guess it's because I have no pedigree and
no fashion fishbone to pick that this tale is mine to tell. So here's all
you need to know about us catwalk cats....

Let's begin at home: the Village. Two floors, curvy
staircase, outdoor terrace, trellises, roof deck. A climber's delight.
And we do love to scale the heights (save for Baby, whose K2 is the
refrigerator). City days are spent having our hair done by Father
when he's not working in Japan; or doing Mother's hair ourselves—
she loves a good clawing out—when she's not working in Vienna or

Brazil. When they're away we take siestas in the sunlight, leap and claw at the fancy rugs, and make small talk with the neighbors. Oh, the gossip between brownstones! Has Donna organized moonlight yoga on her roof? What would net us an invitation to Oscar's for some topiary hide-and-seek? Has Calvin come back from fishing in

Rio with tasty Bahian shrimps? It's rather dishy up near the chimneys: Mother and Father don't know the half of what goes on. When the owner's away ... need I elaborate?

More often than not, however, all seven of us can be found bouncing between Paris, London, and Milan, dashing dizzyingly from shoot to shoot. Henri is useless on set. He likes nothing more than to curl up on the location bus and yammer for hours about the good old days to whoever will listen. (Remember the days before

Young Puff, Wainscott. Spring

Baby & Coco, Wainscott. Christmas

we could text? Before Naomi bought a
cell phone? Why did Claudia date David
Copperfield? And Linda's red hair:
What was she thinking? Who knows?

Who cares?) Baby, meanwhile, is rubbing

up against the security guard in the hopes of getting her paws

on some Fred Leighton chandeliers. (As if.) Coco endlessly

schmoozes the talent—Natalia, Gisele, that Mother-and-me

doppelgänger Karen Elson—trading the secrets of her sashimi diet

for a brush with stardom. Bart gets picked up and handed around

like the latest Marc Jacobs It-bag by all the pretty girls. Youth has

its privileges. Me? I keep an eye on the trunks and sniffily slope

off to a corner every time "Crazy in Love" comes over the sound

system (paws over ears! Can we please stop partying like it's 2004?).

Occasionally I check the Polaroids, keeping my meows to myself.

(If Patrick or Mario or Arthur wants my point of view, I'm happy to oblige. Add a big smile. Lose the hat. Why the curly hair, Dad? Why the lacy leggings, Mom? Honestly, it's not brain science.)

And then there are the collections, our version of the Grand Tour. Here's where all of us cats show our true stripes. Henri has barely a whisker of interest in the runway these days. In Paris he'd rather hole up at Davé or the Ritz Bar or, best of all, Kaspia; don't ask the price, he's never even seen the bill. Sure, he's front-row at Yohji and Comme des Garçons because he's got that artistic soul that respects a longtime visionary. But lift his furry butt for Undercover? Forget it. We don't even see Coco in Paris;

she zips about, collecting her personal orders from Lanvin, Balenciaga, and Rochas. Has never met a sample she didn't like, that one. (I occasionally buy her a swan's down puff—pun

Puff, Wainscott. Autumn

Puff, Wainscott. Spring

unavoidable—from Carita as a gift, because you can never give a fashion girl clothes.) Baby heads straight for Chanel, where these days she's obsessing over cell-phone charms with an intensity of concentration that is frankly embarrassing. (Lose weight and wear the clothes, babe; Karl wrote the book on it....) As for me: J'adore Paris. Bart and I help Father muss the scrawny boys' hair at Dior. We do a drive-by at Colette—great name!—to see if there are any new cat toys in the ground-floor vitrines. We sniff around the heels of Carine Roitfeld and Valentino for invites to after-show shindigs.

After Europe, we're all desperate for the country. So it's off to Wainscott for some lazy days in the sun. Father and I garden for hours. Bart hides in the ferns. Baby nibbles sweet corn. Coco contemplates the

pool. Henri oils his board. Mother cooks. It's quiet and calm, and not the Hamptons you read about. No parties, no clubs, no private movie screenings. I have my own crowd there, MY cat pack. I just wander off for hours to my own secret retreats. It freaks out Mother and Father so much that once, when I "disappeared," they called up a psychic who was able, just by speaking to Mom on the phone, to sense my movements in Long Island. This is the same psychic who told them that Coco has issues with my unclassy roots.

Maybe she's right. Maybe Coco does look down her whiskers at me. But I have two things to say. We all adore each other, hissing or no hissing. And what kind of cat isn't a little bit catty? Mother and Father get this, and get the fact that each of us has our own personality and our own bag of tricks—and that there's a lot

of stuff we keep to ourselves. I guess what I'm saying is that being

chic means having your secrets—playing it a little cat and mouse,

having your own mysterious agenda. So although you're going to

learn a lot about our family in these pages, you're never going to

know everything. Why Mother once dyed a bunch of other cats

lavender for a story; why Father loves hair down and Mother hair

up; or exactly what us fluffy children are thinking when we're

nibbling anchovies in the first-class lounge at Malpensa. But there's

one thing we can't keep secret, and that's scrawled all over these

pages: love, Love, LOVE.

Puff, as told to Sally Singer

GALLERY

Photographs by Didier Malige

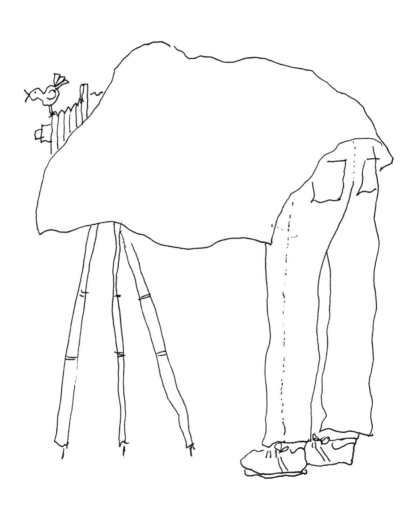

Bart, West 11th Street Terrace. Spring

Puff, Wainscott. Spring

Puff, Wainscott. Autumn

Young Puff, Wainscott. Spring

Bart's First Day, Wainscott. Spring

Coco, NYC. Winter

Henri, Wainscott. Spring

Young Puff, Wainscott. Spring

Coco, Wainscott. Summer

Coco & Henri, NYC. Winter

Bart's First Breakfast.

Wainscott. Spring

Coco & Henri, Wainscott. Autumn

Bart, NYC. Winter

Gardening Puff

Biker Puff

Yoga Puff

Relaxing Puff

Bart, Wainscott. Summer

Henri & Puff, Wainscott. Summer

Bart, Wainscott. Summer

Henri, Wainscott. Summer

Bart, Wainscott. Autumn

I
SPRING

...IN WHICH BART JOINS THE FAMILY;

HELMUT LANG SENDS VALENTINE'S CHOCOLATES;

BABY LEARNS TO FLAMENCO IN SEVILLE;

PUFF COLLECTS AN OSCAR;

AND THE MET BALL CAUSES CATFIGHTS
OVER BIG-NIGHT GLAMOUR.

Little boy Bart — born 6th March 2004

...There were a few hisses when he first arrived, but soon everyone grew to love him....

Don't be silly Bart, I'm not your Dad,
I'm your Uncle Puff — can't you see
I'm a red cat, not a grey cat....?

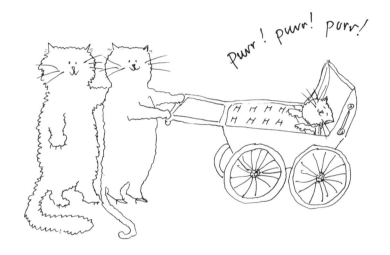

Purr! purr! purr!

I'm sorry Coco, but don't you think our little Bart is rather young to wear Hermès.....?

All the young kittens in
the neighborhood came
over to meet him · · · ·

· · · · · careful in
those high heels
Lilly, don't drop
him !

They all took turns holding him
and thought he was very, very cute....

Unfortunately Bart developed ringworm
soon after he arrived and had to be shaved...

...the same thing had happened a few
years back when Puff arrived so we all
knew the drill .....

Here we go again guys, a bad haircut . . . . .

. . . and stinky baths once a week for six weeks . . . . . GREAT !!

The time soon passed and things
got back to normal .....

.... please Puff Puff, read me another
bedtime story .....

So Little Boy — this is how you have to do Mother's hair... first you comb it through really really well with your claws fully extended......

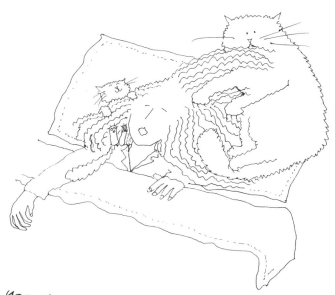

...then you chew it for a while and work up a lot of drool so it becomes quite soggy... by morning it will be all beautiful and curly — oh yes don't forget to purr really loud ... mother loves that...

Don't cry Bart, I'm sure you will get a Valentine card soon ....

... I just can't believe it Baby...those chocolates were mother's Valentine from Helmut Lang...and you ate them all ....

....come on Coco.... just one little kiss for Valentine's day...

Wow! Puff you are such a romantic...

..... girls, girls — I just can't take all this licking....

.... sorry Henri, I ate all your tulips.....!

At first Coco and Puff were always fighting....

....but their relationship soon grew into ....

... a strong and bonding love — and they
became enyaged to be marvied....

...girls bachelorette night at home.

boys bachelor night out .....

coco and Puff were married in New York City.

Afterwards they flew to Saint Barths for their honeymoon.

Coco, I think Patrick Demarchelier invited us over for drinks, but I couldn't really understand a word he was saying .....

Later they were joined in Venice by
the rest of the family....

....this is the life
Bart ... can you
go a little bit
faster....?

BAUER HOTEL
★ ★ ★ ★ ★
V E N E Z I A

Coco Guggenheim !

Next stop India ...

.... honestly Paff, I don't think we can take him back to Long Island as our pet... he just won't fit on the aeroplane .....

RAJVILĀS
JAIPUR

AN OBEROI HOTEL

...so coco, would you
like some more
curried mouse...?

...actually Puff
I prefer the Bombay
duck...!

Goner Road, Jaipur 303 012, India. Telephone (91-141) 64 0101. Facsimile (91-141) 64 0202. Website: http://www.oberoihotels.com

A member of *The Leading Hotels of the World*

.... then on to Spain .

Baby loved the
flamenco dresses, she
felt they disguised her
fuller figure ...

Puff was a little foolhardy,
he forgot that he was a
red cat and tried to have a
conversation with a very
large bull .....

... we all got home just in time for Easter

.... that's really funny Puff but don't you think you should set a good example for Bart and come to church with Henri and me...?

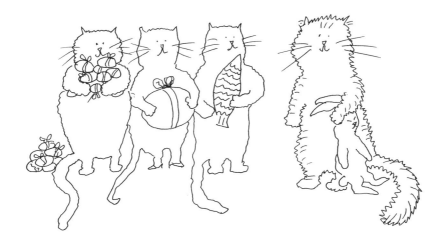

.... oh dear Puff .... I don't think that is what Mother meant when she said .... "go find the Easter bunny ...."

yum! yum!

In April it was Mother's birthday... Baby and Puff baked a huge cake.....

... and there was a very big party at Mr Chow's — every cool cat in town was there to celebrate.

There are many, many parties in Springtime ....

Puff spends hours in front of the mirror
getting his 'look' just right .....

Oscar Night — Puff got "Best Cat" award
for his role in Gladiator ....

.... my Lords, ladies and gentlemen...
I want to thank everyone for this wonderful
honor — thank you Coco for all your loving advice,
thank you Henri for teaching me the rules of the
game, thank you Baby for keeping me on my
muscle-building, fighter's diet, thank you Stripy
and all the cats in Wainscott Woods for showing
me how to fight dirty ... and win. I also want
to thank Mother for always being there
when I get beat up, and
Father for training me so
well together with my
sparring partner Bart.
Thank you Luz for
taking such good care
of us all when our parents
are away ... and thank you
Kuba and Tyson and my
neighbors Lilly and Stretch and
Scarlett and Sparky ... and
thank you Lolo for writing my speech ....

And the party of the year is the Costume Institute
Gala at the Metropolitan Museum ....

The Goddess 2003

.... sorry Coco but
Nicole Kidman is
going to be mad
when she sees
you in her
Gucci dress ...

Dangerous Liaisons 2004

.... oh Puff, how am I
going to sit down for dinner
.... my dress has a
Watteau back ....?

Anglomania 2006

... didn't I just see
Drew Barrymore wearing
that same Dior dress,
Baby .... ?

Hussein
Chalayan

Alexander
McQueen

Vivienne Westwood

II
SUMMER

…IN WHICH DAVÉ TELLS PUFF'S FORTUNE;

COCO AND BABY SHOP THE COUTURE;

HENRI SURFS WITH DAVID SIMS IN
THE HAMPTONS WHILE TACKLING
CATNIP ADDICTION;

AND A CHOPPER RIDE WHISKS
A HOMESICK CITY CAT BACK TO
GREENWICH VILLAGE.

Summer always starts with a trip to Paris...

...oh dear Henri — do you think our Pet-trac
micro-chips will set off the X-ray machine ...?

Jean-Louis, their long time driven
picked them up from the airport and
took them to the Ritz Hotel ... after
they had unpacked they all went
sight seeing ....

Ritz Paris

The "tour de France"

Puff is hoping one day he will
beat Lance Armstrong.... -

Ritz Paris 15. Place Vendôme 75041 Paris Cedex 01

TÉLÉPHONE (33) 01 43 16 30 30 - E-MAIL MANAGEMENT : mgt@ritzparis.com - E-MAIL RÉSERVATION resa@ritzparis.com
TÉLÉFAX RÉSERVATION (33) 01 43 16 36 68 / 01 43 16 36 69 - TÉLÉFAX (33) 01 43 16 31 78 / 01 43 16 31 79 - RCS PARIS B 572 219 913 - SIRET 572 219 913 00017

Dinner chez "Davé"

... we have our polaroid taken to
put up on his wall of celebrities ....
afterwards Davé tells our fortunes ....

TÉLÉPHONE (33) 01 43 16 30 30 - E-MAIL MANAGEMENT : mgt@ritzparis.com - E-MAIL RÉSERVATION resa@ritzparis.com
TÉLÉFAX RÉSERVATION (33) 01 43 16 36 68 / 01 43 16 36 69 - TÉLÉFAX (33) 01 43 16 31 78 / 01 43 16 31 79 - RCS PARIS B 572 219 913 - SIRET 572 219 913 00017

Puff always gets a good front row

seat next to all the most important editors....

... after the shows we had an extravagant shoot inspired by Marie Antoinette....

I adore these Manolos, Annie, and it is an honor to be Kirsten Dunst's stand in ... please don't chop off my head for suggesting this, but are you really sure she wants to be nude ...?

.... meanwhile Puff had to rush over to Germany as his book was going to press....

...so Gerhard have you published many cat books before ours....?

Ritz Paris

... back in Paris Coco and Baby went for their

couture fittings ... Baby loved a beautiful pink Balmain
dress by Oscar de la Renta while coco preferred this little
20's chemise from Chanel.

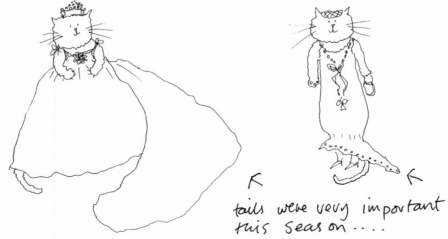

tails were very important
this season ....

Ritz Paris 15, Place Vendôme 75041 Paris Cedex 01

TÉLÉPHONE (33) 01 43 16 30 30 - E-MAIL MANAGEMENT : mgt@ritzparis.com - E-MAIL RÉSERVATION resa@ritzparis.com

TÉLÉFAX RÉSERVATION (33) 01 43 16 36 68 / 01 43 16 36 69 - TÉLÉFAX (33) 01 43 16 31 78 / 01 43 16 31 79 - RCS PARIS B 572 219 913 - SIRET 572 219 913 00017

Ritz Paris

...all together they did so much shopping they couldn't get their large Louis Vuitton suitcase to close...

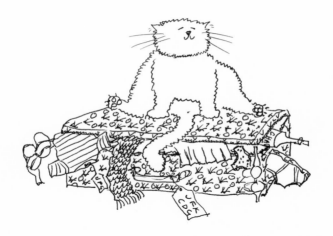

....even when Bart sat on it ...so they asked Fiona in their Paris office to Fedex it home for them ....

Ritz Paris 15, Place Vendôme 75041 Paris Cedex 01
TÉLÉPHONE (33) 01 43 16 30 30 - E-MAIL MANAGEMENT : mgt@ritzparis.com - E-MAIL RÉSERVATION resa@ritzparis.com
TÉLÉFAX RÉSERVATION (33) 01 43 16 36 68 / 01 43 16 36 69 - TÉLÉFAX (33) 01 43 16 31 78 / 01 43 16 31 79 - RCS PARIS B 572 219 913 - SIRET 572 219 913 00017

After all that work everyone was ready for the summer holidays in the Hamptons...

.....even though there is usually a lot of traffic on the L.I.E. they love to drive — they like to wave at all the other cats in their S.U.V.'s and Hummers .....

.... the first thing Baby likes to do, when we arrive, is stock up the fridge with lots of juicy young mice ... So Puff gets busy hunting. . . .

..... unfortunately he usually returns home covered
with ticks ....

If it is not too windy, Father takes us all sailing in his boat called "Grace".

Bert has to wear his water-wings in case he falls over board ... Sometimes he is a little bit clumsy and misses his step ....

.... poor coco often gets sea-sick ....

During the summer Puff decided to write our family's biography...

.... so Lolo you would be purrfect to ghostwrite my book ....

.... good gracious Puff , I can't believe
Mr Penn actually photographed your great
grandfather and made a print for you....

one day Puff wandered down to Easthampton
beach and suddenly found himself modeling
for an Arthur Elgort fashion shoot.

..--. meanwhile Henri went
surfing with his new friend
David Sims.

after that, Puff and Bart hung out at the beach everyday .... they were happy to run into Mario Testino who immediately offered them a job.....

.... I was thinking, you are so goodlooking Puff, it would be great for you to be my sixth assistant, and Bart could be my runner ....

Wow Baby your Robo-cat is really cute... ...yes coco he keeps bringing me lots of mice...

...inspired by Puff's success with Arthur, Coco and Baby
wove over to Westbury Gardens where Steven Klein was
hooting a lead story for September Vogue.....

Baby's absolute favorite summer dish
is sweetcorn ... she loves when it is
all buttery.....

careful Bart — I know you want to catch your first bird, but there are easier ways .... trust me!

Bart's favorite summer occupation is climbing trees .... the trouble is he often gets stuck ....

Bart fell in the swimming
pool twice during the summer
... needless to say he was not
wearing his water-wings so
Puff had to jump in and
rescue him .....

Henri has a bit of a
problem with his addiction
to cat-nip ... he gets very
depressed in the winter time,
when it all dies down ....

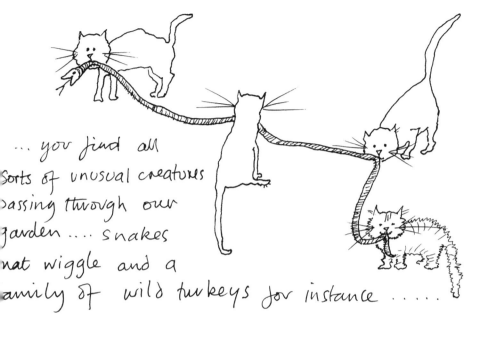

... you find all
sorts of unusual creatures
passing through our
garden .... snakes
that wiggle and a
family of wild turkeys for instance .....

.... I thought I counted 5 young turkeys last
night Bart .....?

... the girls decided to go over and visit Cassidy who was staying with Helmut and Edward and their cat Kuba ...

.... they had a bit of a problem with the ducks and chickens ... who laughed at their rather old fashioned swimsuits...

How do I look Ralph?

... late in August the boys got quite sporty... Henri went over to Bridgehampton for a game of polo .....

.... while Puff went for a spin on the back of Craig McDean's 1962 Triumph Tiger ....

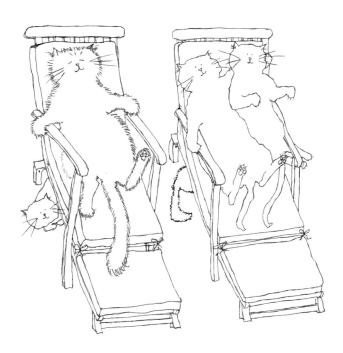

.... best of all we like to take a snooze, at
the end of the day, until we are called
in for our dinner ....

At the end of the summer Puff gets restless,
he is anxious to get back to the city and work ...
.... so he takes the helicopter from Easthampton
air port ...

III
AUTUMN

…IN WHICH THE CATS DROOPILY
RETURN TO WORK;

COURT STARDOM IN
BRUCE WEBER'S EXHIBITION;

MAKE A SPLASH ON THE
CHANEL CATWALK;

AND MODEL THE TRENDS
FOR A VERY FURRY FALL.

It is so windy in the Autumn . . . . .
. . . This leaf sweeping is driving
me crazy . . . .

.....it is often extremely windy on our terrace also.....
one day our umbrella took off and Puff gallantly
tried to save it......

...so listen up Stretch and Lilly — I want to establish one thing at this condominium meeting...

...you two are in charge of the garden ..... absolutely no dogs are allowed ...except, of course, Scarlett and Sparky ....

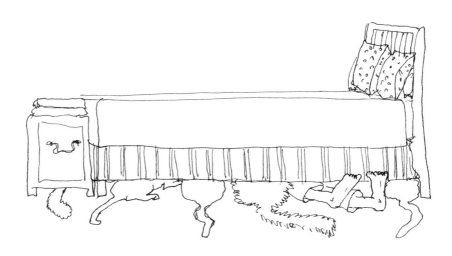

.... when the time comes to go back to work
we all hide under the bed ......

...wait for me guys — I'll get lost alone on the subway.....

oh my goodness Henri — where is Bart ?

.. have we lost him AGAIN .... ?!

phew Puff! how cool ... we are in Bruce Weber's
exhibition, we are going to be famous .....

.... do you think other cats will ask
for our autographs now, coco?

At Bruce's movie premiere.....

I'm so sorry Coco - Tyson told me this film - "A letter to True" - was all about <u>cats</u>, not dogs....

Good grief Baby
you bought the same
Dean Harris earrings
as Phyllis ... you can't
wear those in Paris
she will be furious...

Getting ready for the collections is quite a
production — we all check our wardrobes....

.... and try out some
new, cool hair do's....

Louis, the "King of colour" will take good care
of you Mr Puff ... would you like to stay
with hed ......?

.... the usual Puff Puff — a little "Vamp" on
your claws and we will leave them really
long .... OK?

FOUR SEASONS HOTEL
Milano
A FOUR SEASONS · REGENT HOTEL

We arrive in Milan after a long flight...

...and rush right over to Bice, with all the other fashion cats ... for a delicious plate of pasta with tartuffo

VIA GESÙ 6/8 - 20121 MILANO - ITALIA - TELEFONO (+39) 0277088 FAX (+39) 027708 5000 - WORLD WIDE WEB: www.fourseasons.com
REGENT MILANO S.p.A. - Sede Sociale: Via Gesù, 6/8 - 20121 Milano - Telefono (+39) 0277088 - Fax (+39) 027708 5000
Capitale Sociale: € 15.000.000,00 i.v. - Codice Fiscale, Partita IVA, Registro Imprese 03738430960 - Tribunale di Milano - R.E.A. Milano 1698130
DEFINING THE ART OF SERVICE AT 60 HOTELS IN 29 COUNTRIES

.... we soon realise all our outfits look
old fashioned ... nothing but grey cat-suits ... ugh!

... so we hurry over to Corso Como
and then to Fendi for a lovely new
fur coat .....

VIA GESÙ 6/8 - 20121 MILANO - ITALIA - TELEFONO (+39) 0277088 FAX (+39) 027708 5000 - WORLD WIDE WEB: www.fourseasons.com
REGENT MILANO S.p.A. - Sede Sociale: Via Gesù, 6/8 - 20121 Milano - Telefono (+39) 0277088 - Fax (+39) 027708 5000
Capitale Sociale: € 15.000.000,00 i.v. - Codice Fiscale, Partita IVA, Registro Imprese 03738430960 - Tribunale di Milano - R.E.A. Milano 1698130
DEFINING THE ART OF SERVICE AT 60 HOTELS IN 29 COUNTRIES

FOUR SEASONS HOTEL
Milano
A FOUR SEASONS · REGENT HOTEL

.... we shopped
until we .....

.... dropped ...

... do you think it is
politically correct for a
cat to wear fur, loco?
I· do hope we don't run
into those PETA people...

VIA GESÙ 6/8 - 20121 MILANO - ITALIA - TELEFONO (+39) 0277088 FAX (+39) 027708 5000 - WORLD WIDE WEB: www.fourseasons.com
REGENT MILANO S.p.A. - Sede Sociale: Via Gesù, 6/8 - 20121 Milano - Telefono (+39) 0277088 - Fax (+39) 027708 5000
Capitale Sociale: € 15.000.000,00 i.v. - Codice Fiscale, Partita IVA, Registro Imprese 03738430960 - Tribunale di Milano - R.E.A. Milano 1698130
DEFINING THE ART OF SERVICE AT 60 HOTELS IN 29 COUNTRIES

.... not all the trends
for fall are easy to wear...

... very long pants for instance
are difficult to walk in...

... big shoulder pads are not
for everyone – they tend to
make your head look small...

.... and no cat over
six months old should
wear a mini skirt...

VIA GESÙ 6/8 - 20121 MILANO - ITALIA - TELEFONO (+39) 0277088 FAX (+39) 027708 5000 - WORLD WIDE WEB: www.fourseasons.com
REGENT MILANO S.p.A. - Sede Sociale: Via Gesù, 6/8 - 20121 Milano - Telefono (+39) 0277088 - Fax (+39) 027708 5000
Capitale Sociale: € 15.000.000,00 i.v. - Codice Fiscale, Partita IVA, Registro Imprese 03738430960 - Tribunale di Milano - R.E.A. Milano 1698130
DEFINING THE ART OF SERVICE AT 60 HOTELS IN 29 COUNTRIES

Ritz Paris

.... when we got to Paris we called Helmut Lang for a preview ... his collection was really, really edgy .....

Ritz Paris 15. Place Vendôme 75041 Paris Cedex 01

TÉLÉPHONE (33) 01 43 16 30 30 - E-MAIL MANAGEMENT : mgt@ritzparis.com - E-MAIL RÉSERVATION resa@ritzparis.com

TÉLÉFAX RÉSERVATION (33) 01 43 16 36 68 / 01 43 16 36 69 - TÉLÉFAX (33) 01 43 16 31 78 / 01 43 16 31 79 - RCS PARIS B 572 219 913 - SIRET 572 219 913 00017

Ritz Paris

Yohji did a great wedding dress ... Baby has
been looking for a husband ever since ....

Ritz Paris 15. Place Vendôme 75041 Paris Cedex 01

TÉLÉPHONE (33) 01 43 16 30 30 - E-MAIL MANAGEMENT : mgt@ritzparis.com - E-MAIL RÉSERVATION resa@ritzparis.com

TÉLÉFAX RÉSERVATION (33) 01 43 16 36 68 / 01 43 16 36 69 - TÉLÉFAX (33) 01 43 16 31 78 / 01 43 16 31 79 - RCS PARIS B 572 219 913 - SIRET 572 219 913 00017

Since Karl is our special friend, he invited us to
... we got a lot of press and had to have

make a guest appearance on his runway at Chanel
"security" for the rest of our trip ....!

When we got home we had to do our "Collections" shoot.

woof woof - I've been on the cover of ..

....production, production — can we get this dog,
Vida, out of here, she is upsetting the 'talent'....

We took a chance on using Kuba as our model — she is rather young.

Bruce and Nan's cat, Tyson, came over to lend a paw....
needless to say he brought an elephant and wanted
Kuba to do a nude .....

..Steven Meisel lent Puff his lucky hat.. Yumi, go powder Kuba's nose.

Balenciaga

Louis vuitton

Y.S.L.

Prada

Rochas

McQueen

Louis Vuitton

Balenciaga

coco likes to edit the photographs a bit before
we send them into the magazine.....

...this cat looks too young Puff

no Puff no.... too scratchy

this cat is too fat

too meowy

this cat is too thin

no no no Puff

too snarly

why can't all the cats
be purring?

too hissy

I hate marmalade
cats ... we need more
black cats...

I'm sorry Puff...it is a reshoot----the fur was too fluffy...

... don't purr too loud Puff ... Father has a bit of a headache after our reshoot .....

.... all those cats in the Tim Walker photograph
that Father bought, look just like you Bart –
you'd better be careful he doesn't get any ideas
to colour you lavender too ....

.... you know what Puff...if it wasn't for your big fluffy tail, you just might have gotten away with it ......

Every year we go to the Halloween Parade
on 6th Avenue.

.... stop jumping up and down Bart, you are
making me dizzy... I can hardly see which
way to go inside this pumpkin as it is .....

a toilet brush ?   a pout ?   a cobweb brush ?

a hair ball ?   a broom ?   a dreadlock wig ?

... ours is a multi-talented family, first
Bart got the Calvin Klein underwear campaign

... then Puff was elected Governor of New York
... now he has his eye set on the White House ...

IV
WINTER

... IN WHICH PUFF AND THE FAMILY
DEVOUR SUSHI AND PRADA;

TAKE IN THE SIGHTS OF TOKYO,
JAMAICA, AND MUMBAI;

MEET SANTA CLAUS AT MARC'S;

AND FEAST ON NATALIA'S
CHRISTMAS CAVIAR.

.... I think we should just leave the cooking to
Puff and Baby this Thanksgiving Coco....

oops!

.... maybe you should throw up a few more
fur balls, Coco, you ate so much dinner...

phew!

sorry Bart, I don't think even you are going to get those Hedi Slimane pants done up....

... twice a week Luz comes to give us our spanish lessons ....

... come to Luz little Bart,
would you like to watch
some more Spanish T.V. ...?

.... this is my favorite pair
of shoes ... I do wish Father
wouldn't take them away
and wear them
every day .....

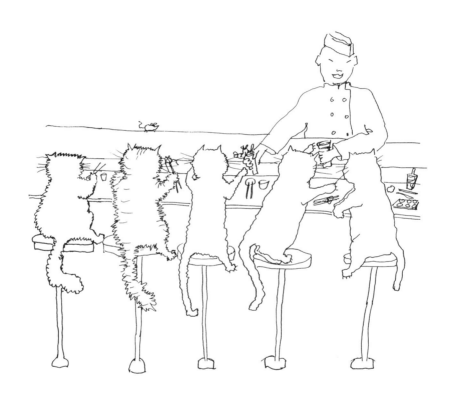

Yuki-san always makes us something
special when we go to Zutto for dinner...

sorry guys, we loved your Prada coats so we
got some too....please don't call us copy-cats!

We decided to launch our new book in Japan....

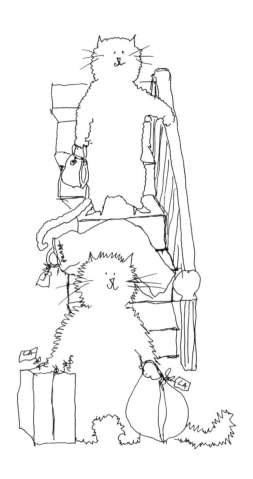

... so we packed our bags and made all the appropriate arrangements....

...on the way there we stopped at Honolulu...

... at the airport the girls were given some beautiful leis .... they were very daring and went topless .....

Hotel Okura
TOKYO

In Tokyo...

Bart got a few good wrestling tips
from his new Sumo friend...

2-10-4 Toranomon · Minato-ku · Tokyo 105-0001 · Japan · Telephone:(03)3582-0111 · Facsimile:(03)3582-3707

Hotel Okura
TOKYO

Rei Kawakubo threw us a party in her
comme des Garçons shop to celebrate
our book.....

2-10-4 Toranomon · Minato-ku · Tokyo 105-0001 · Japan · Telephone:(03)3582-0111 · Facsimile:(03)3582-3707

Round Hill
HOTEL AND VILLAS

.... after the party, did we need a holiday?!
...not until we got to Jamaica did we start
to relax .....

Round Hill
HOTEL AND VILLAS

...you'll never believe it Mother — I met this really cool black cat, he took us all out to a reggae club and I didn't even get into a fight.......

P.O. Box 64, Montego Bay, Jamaica, W.I. • Telephone: (809) 952-5150-5 • Fax: (809) 952-2505 • Res.: (800) 972-2159

... when we returned we all had to go to the Saint Marks vet for one thing or another....

Henri hurt his arm...

Baby had to have a tooth out ....

coco went on "the pill", and she needed fluid as she was dehydrated by the long flight home.

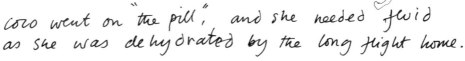

... after his "operation" Bart had to have therapy with Christine our pet psychic...

Puff, Puff ... where have they gone ...?

... later poor Coco had to stay at the vet's for three weeks because she was radio-active after her thyroid treatment ....

Puff developed some "funny turns" and had
to go to the big Animal Hospital for a M.R.I.

oh Dr Place I'm feeling all woozy, I think
I am in love ... may I call you Beverly ...?

... and Bart had a lot of problems with his stomach after all his travels, but Dr Kuroski soon took care of that.....

It soon got much colder so Puff borrowed Mother's new fur hat from Prada....

... predictably he got called some rather mean names by the local cats in Wainscott woods...

... after which he required a visit to Dr Browning for a bit of a "clean up"...

...so we all built an enormous snow-cat in the garden...

.... then we went
skating on Easthampton
pond ....

some of us were
quite good ....

.... and some
were not ....!

Bart told Santa
all the things
he would like
for Christmas...

.... the list
was endless....

Bart went to bed early on Christmas eve...

.... he wanted to be sure Santa
would not forget him ....

Santa invited Bart over to the
Marc Jacobs store where he was

staying during Christmas, as the North Pole
is so far away from New York .....

···· Christmas morning ···

... quickly Coco, open
up Joe's present — remember
last year he gave you all that
sexy underwear ...!

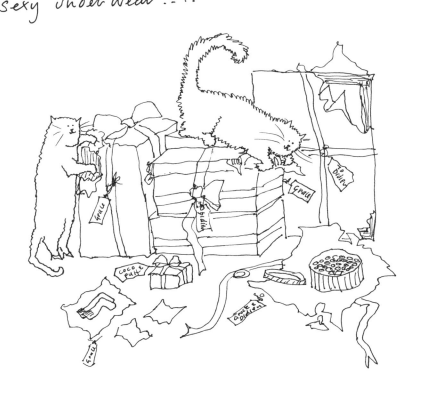

Natalia sent us
all a big box of
caviar from Russia....

Puff wanted to kiss
all the girls under
the mistletoe ....

... but he was
quickly distracted
by the turkey!

...after dinner Puff
had a cigar, while Bart
tried on his present from Santa.

.... by the end of the
day everyone was a bit tipsy....

Puff and Bart sang a duet by the fireside

.... please don't sing too loud Bart, you will upset our neighbor and he will start to bang on the ceiling again ....

.... at the end of the evening, Coco and Puff took Rudolf for a walk before bed....

..... and so to sleep.

THANK YOU

Anna Wintour, Franca Sozzani, Carine Roitfeld, Suzy Menkes, André Leon Talley,
Drew Barrymore, Kirsten Dunst, Lance Armstrong, Natalia Vodianova, Phyllis Posnick, Fiona Da Rin,
Davé, Louis Licari, Yuki at Zutto, Jean-Louis Lederlé, Tristan Rigby, Brian Fee, Sophie Griffiths,
Joyce Rubin, Caroline Jackson, Bonnie Sheldon, Juan Rodriguez, Anna Piaggi, Isabella Blow

Manolo Blahnik, Ralph Lauren, John Galliano, Stephen Jones, Alexander McQueen, Miuccia Prada, Helmut Lang,
Edward Pavlick, Yohji Yamamoto, Marc Jacobs, Calvin Klein, Rei Kawakubo, Nicolas Ghesquière, Olivier Theyskens,
Hedi Slimane, Dean Harris, Stefano Pilati, Jean-Paul Gaultier, Oscar de la Renta, Hussein Chalayan, Vivienne Westwood

Arthur Elgort, Steven Klein, Mario Testino, David Sims, Irving Penn, Craig McDean,
Bruce Weber & Nan Bush, Steven Meisel, Patrick Demarchelier, Tim Walker, Annie Leibovitz

Josiane Malige, Annette Gallopin, Chantal Duques, Antoinette Ingrain, Marie Madeleine Besnard,
Andre Rebiffe and family, Pierre Leroux, Frédéric Fekkai, Chelsea Black and White Labs,
Charly Griffin, Joe McKenna, Nicoletta Santoro, Palma Driscoll, and all the photographers
who have inspired Didier to take pictures

Dr. Sally Haddock, Dr. Amy Kurowski, Dr. Beverly Place, Dr. Barry Browning,
Dr. Mark Davis, Christine Agro

Karl Lagerfeld, Gerhard Steidl

First edition 2006. © 2006 Edition 7L. © 2006 for text and drawings by Grace Coddington. Photographs: Didier Malige. Book design: Michael Roberts. Printing: Steidl, Göttingen.
Steidl, Düstere Strasse 4, D-37073 Göttingen Phone +49 551 49 60 60, Fax +49 551 49 60 649 E-mail mail@steidl.de www.steidlville.com / www.steidl.de.
Orders can be placed directly at our publishing house or via e-mail ISBN 3-86521-344-8 ISBN 13: 978-3-86521-344-0. Printed in Germany